ISBN: 978-0-8203-6244-1

View more work by Alan Reid at *www.alanreid.design*.

Printed in Canada

This book was produced by the Little Cumberland Island Homeowners Association in support of the U.S. Fish and Wildlife Service, which funded construction of a living shoreline on the banks of Shell Creek within the Cumberland Island National Seashore. For more information, visit *littlecumberlandisland.com*.

THIS BOOK IS SPONSORED AND SUPPORTED BY:
The Georgia Department of Natural Resources
Georgia Southern University
Little Cumberland Island Science, Research, and Conservation Committee
The Nature Conservancy
The University of Georgia's Odum School of Ecology

THIS BOOK WOULD NOT EXIST WITHOUT THE SUPPORT OF THE FOLLOWING PEOPLE:
Jordan Dodson, *Georgia Department of Natural Resources*
Dr. Paula Eubanks, *Little Cumberland Island Living Shoreline Committee*
Dr. Chester W. Jackson, *Georgia Southern University, Geology and Geography*
Daniel Harris, *University of Georgia, Odum School of Ecology*
Jamie King, *Georgia Department of Natural Resources*
Christi Lambert, *The Nature Conservancy*
Jan Mackinnon, *Georgia Department of Natural Resources*
Lexie Parker, *Little Cumberland Island Living Shoreline Committee*
Dr. Russell Regnery, *Little Cumberland Island Science, Research, and Conservation Committee*
Dr. Heather C. Scott, *Georgia Southern University, College of Education*
Our child reviewers: **Victor Burkins**, **Eileen Preston**, and **Elijah Stone**

A percentage of the proceeds from this book support The Carreta Foundation, Inc. This nonprofit organization supports research and conservation on the Georgia coast.

*With love and gratitude for my father, Robert W. Frey (1938–1992),
a geologist and marine scientist who taught me to love
the amazing ecosystem of the Georgia coast.*

— Valerie J. Frey

*To young artists: Your beautiful imagination cannot be envisioned by
another, so use your two hands to tell the rest of us stories of the
wonder and mystery of Earth.*

— Alan Reid

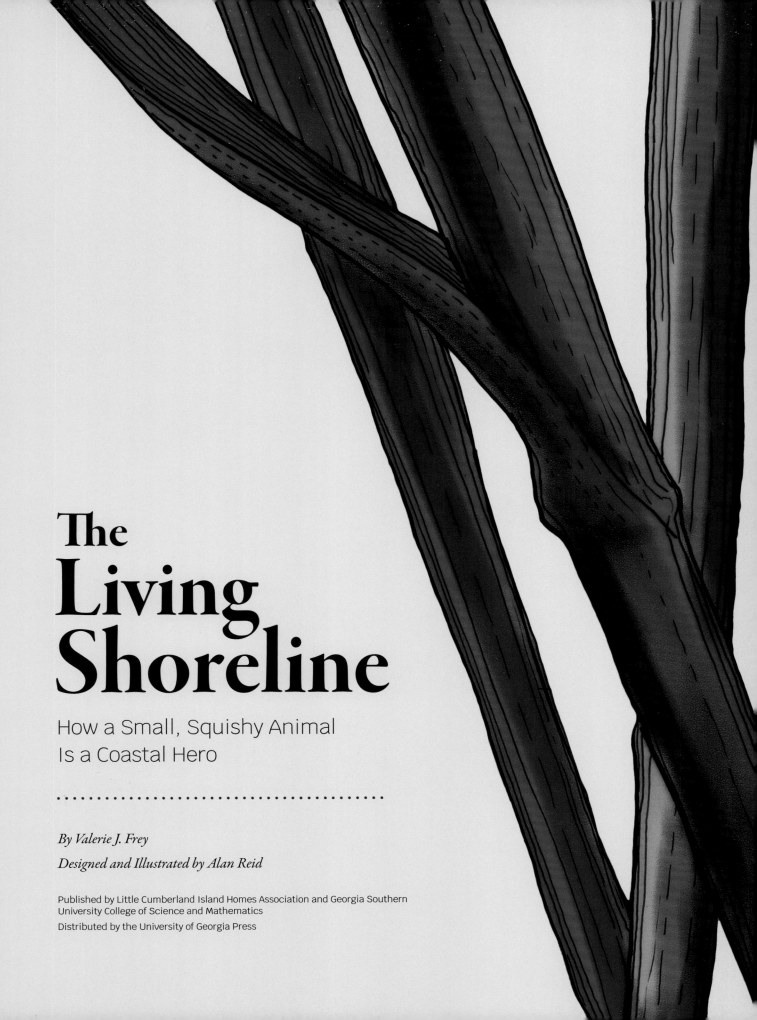

The Living Shoreline

How a Small, Squishy Animal
Is a Coastal Hero

· ·

By Valerie J. Frey

Designed and Illustrated by Alan Reid

Published by Little Cumberland Island Homes Association and Georgia Southern
University College of Science and Mathematics

Distributed by the University of Georgia Press

On a warm evening, you and a buddy
head to a fishing hole along the Georgia coast.

You walk quietly enough that you startle some wild turkeys at the edge of the *live oak* trees. You set a cooler holding a couple of bottles of lemonade in the shade of *wax myrtle* and *Eastern red cedar* trees. Then the two of you follow a sandy path. The rough leaves of *sea oxeye daisies* scratch against your ankles and thumb-sized *fiddler crabs* scuttle out of your way. Then you arrive at a small floating dock on the creek that winds through the salt marsh.

*You're fishing on a **tidal** creek, so twice a day tides raise the water level and then let it drop down again.*

Right now, the tide has just begun to go out, so the ramp to the water isn't steep. Breezes flow over the **Spartina** marsh grass and push white clouds across the sky. A **snowy egret** wading in the muddy edge of the water looks carefully at you before deciding to take off, his long wings beating evenly as he flies away.

You sit down to get your fishing rod ready and bait your hook with a **mud minnow**, noticing the lapping sound of small waves. You also hear the quick, creaky call of a **clapper rail** bird and the "um um ummm" of a **toadfish**.

Occasionally, there is a click from an oyster closing its shell now that the water level is sinking. If you're looking in that direction, you may see a little spurt of water as the shell snaps shut. You and your buddy have good luck, catching **spotted sea trout**, a **red drum**, and a **sheepshead**. That's good enough for one fishing trip!

You slide your feet into the tidal current, wiggling your toes as you sip on your cool lemonade. Feels good, doesn't it? You don't notice that there are tiny dots floating in the water around your feet.

You gather your things and stroll home to enjoy a late supper of fresh fish. **But did you know those floating dots may have made your whole enjoyable fishing trip possible?**

Toadfish

Instead of a person, let's imagine what life would be like if you were one of those floating dots.

You're happily living in the water. You don't need arms or legs, but you're not a fish. You don't even need a nose or eyes. *What are you?*

You are a larva, a very young oyster.

As an oyster, you begin life smaller than the period at the end of this sentence. You drift along for two to three weeks, growing as you ride flowing patterns in the water called currents.

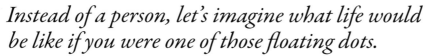

Trochophore   *Veliger*   *Pediveliger*

As a very young human, you were once called an infant. You then grew into a toddler followed by a preschooler. As a very young oyster, you are first a **trochophore** (trok-*uh*-fawr), then a **veliger** (*vee*-li-jer), and finally a **pediveliger** (ped-e-*vee*-li-jer). These words may seem strange, but they describe the awesome things you do as an oyster larva.

Spotted sea trout

Red drum

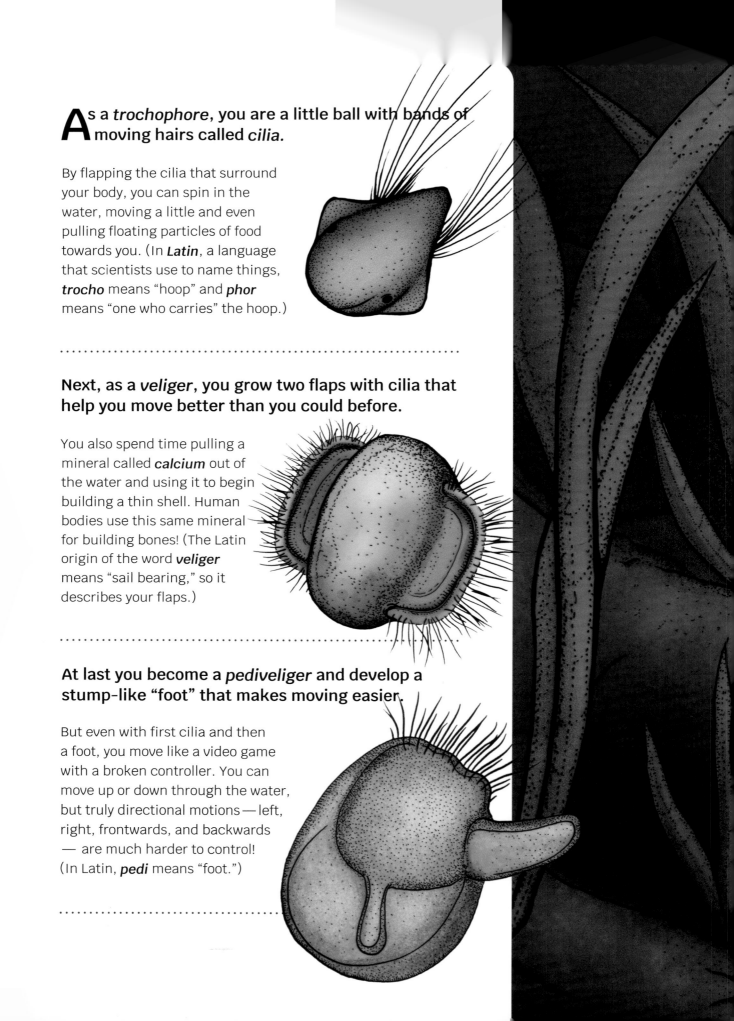

As a *trochophore*, you are a little ball with bands of moving hairs called *cilia.*

By flapping the cilia that surround your body, you can spin in the water, moving a little and even pulling floating particles of food towards you. (In *Latin*, a language that scientists use to name things, *trocho* means "hoop" and *phor* means "one who carries" the hoop.)

Next, as a *veliger*, you grow two flaps with cilia that help you move better than you could before.

You also spend time pulling a mineral called *calcium* out of the water and using it to begin building a thin shell. Human bodies use this same mineral for building bones! (The Latin origin of the word *veliger* means "sail bearing," so it describes your flaps.)

At last you become a *pediveliger* and develop a stump-like "foot" that makes moving easier.

But even with first cilia and then a foot, you move like a video game with a broken controller. You can move up or down through the water, but truly directional motions — left, right, frontwards, and backwards — are much harder to control! (In Latin, *pedi* means "foot.")

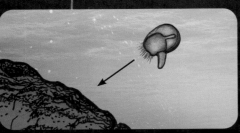

As a human, by the time you were done with your time as a preschooler, you were ready for elementary school. What about as an oyster larva? As your time as a pediveliger draws to a close, it is time to find a place to call home. The "oyster you" will never move from that spot for the rest of your life!

Down through the water you wiggle until eventually you bump into something hard — perhaps part of a pier or old metal pieces from a shipwreck.

More likely, you land on the solid shell of a grown-up oyster. You know exactly what to do. Grab on!

You use calcium as a sort of cement to attach or "set" yourself.

. . . .

Now you are no longer a larva but instead are called an oyster **spat**. Your main jobs are to grow bigger and to build a strong shell that can open and close.

If oysters could talk, perhaps right now you'd like to interrupt:

"Hey, wait a minute. What was that about oysters making the whole fishing adventure possible? And didn't the book title say something about me being a hero?"

The amazing way that oysters get their start is just part of the story. Read on!

As an oyster, you and your fellow oysters don't just live near each other. You often attach yourselves to each other in clumps that form an oyster reef or bed.

In some ways it is like a big, jumbled apartment complex. When new oysters form on the tops and sides of older oysters, the reef grows larger and larger.

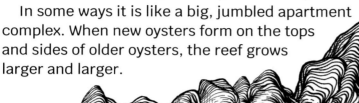

Living clustered together provides **insulation**. Just as the drink cooler you brought on your fishing trip put thick walls between your cold lemonade and the warm air, oysters insulate each other on particularly hot or chilly days.

Now that you are connected to other oysters, you will grow a little like a plant with the narrow part of your shell "rooted" in the most crowded part of the reef and the larger, rounded parts of your shell facing outward so that water can easily flow in. Oysters are **bivalves**. Just as a **bi**cycle has two wheels and **bi**plane has two sets of wings, a **bivalve** has two shells. As an oyster, you need to be able to open your two shells a few millimeters wide to allow water inside.

Diamondback
Terrapin

*Some oysters are **subtidal** and spend their entire lives under the water.*

In Georgia, however, most of our oysters are **intertidal**. As a Georgia oyster, you will live part of your life below water (when the tide is high) and part of your life above the water (when the tide is low). What do you do when the water goes down and you don't want to dry out? You snap your bivalve shells shut. Squirt! As your shells come together, you may spurt out extra water.

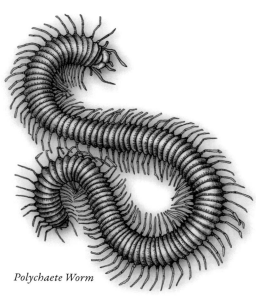

Polychaete Worm

· ·

Every oyster needs to be able to be in the water for part of the day, but some oysters live higher up on the reef while some are lower. The oysters are different ages and sizes. That makes for a lumpy and sprawling oyster reef that is a perfect place for little fish to play hide and seek!

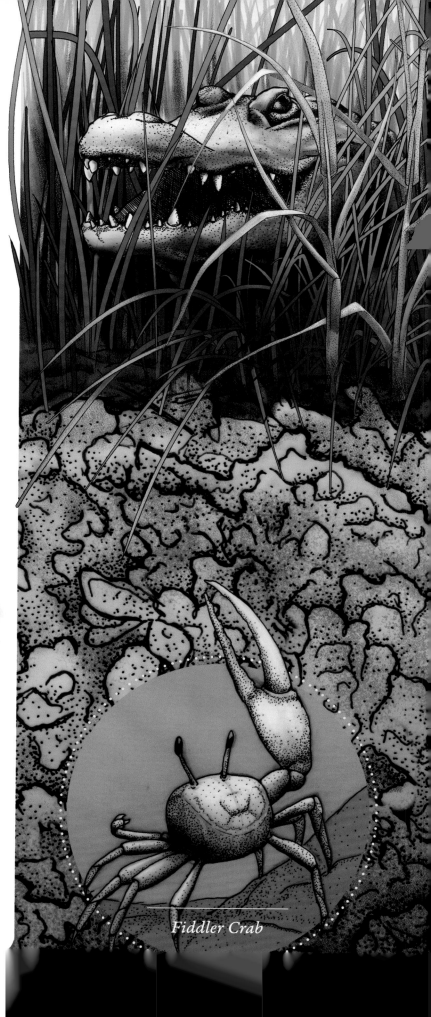

Fiddler Crab

At high tide, your oyster reef with all its nooks and crannies can create safe places for small fish needing to stay away from bigger fish who might eat them. Depending on the water level, small crabs, shrimp, worms, and snails also look for safe spots among oysters that will hide them from shorebirds looking for a meal.

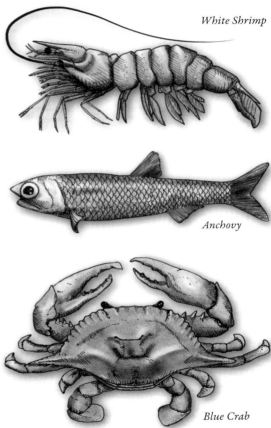

White Shrimp

Anchovy

Blue Crab

Remember the fish the "human you" caught this evening? When those fish were young, underwater oyster beds may have sheltered them long enough so they could grow to the right size for people to catch and enjoy for dinner.

Mummichog

The oyster reef also helps create habitats (natural homes) in more than one way.

When water flows around and through a reef, it bumps into the oyster shells and slows down. **Sediment**, sand and bits of mud swirling in the water, also slows down and drops out of the current to form sandy or muddy patches. These patches around oyster reefs are sheltered spots where other bivalves like clams and mussels can safely live. Snails and worms are happy here too.

Clam

At times, these sandy and muddy patches allow a nice spot where **Spartina** can sprout, grow into marsh grass, and build up the coastal habitat.

When oysters live in clumps, they also make themselves harder to eat!

As an oyster, there are many animals that find you yummy. Remember that fish called a sheepshead that the "human you" caught and had for supper? Now that you're an oyster, he'll want to eat YOU! As a single oyster, part of your shell would easily fit in his mouth. When you're clustered with your oyster friends, however, you are more than a mouthful and there are multiple shells for the sheepshead to wrestle with.

Sheepshead have large teeth that look almost human and they love to crunch open oysters.

What else loves you as a food source?

Animals such as the **sheepshead fish** you caught as well as **rays** will be looking you over when they get hungry. The **toadfish** you heard humming this evening would love you as a snack.

A **boring sponge** is not the uninteresting object you use to clean the dishes but instead is an animal that parks on an oyster and *bores* or drills a hole through its shell so it can eat. One type of marine (saltwater) snail bores holes in oyster shells often enough that its name is the **oysterdrill**.

Oysterdrill

Racoons, **opossums**, and **otters** like to eat oysters as do many birds.

The **American oystercatcher** is a bird that uses piles of old oyster shells called *rakes* or *ridges* as their nesting grounds and their bills are perfectly shaped for opening nearby living oysters.

Gulls also like oysters but have a different way of opening them. If they find a single oyster or oysters in small clusters, they sometimes swoop them high up into the air and then drop them on the ground so the shell breaks to reveal the tender meat inside.

"Ouch," says oyster you!

When you're imagining yourself as an oyster, being eaten sounds terrible. But oysters are an important source of food for many animals.

The salt marsh and **waterways** (creeks and rivers), like all other habitats across planet Earth, have food chains. Plants and small animals are eaten by bigger animals that are in turn eaten by still bigger animals. What is an example of a salt marsh food chain? Tiny water plants called algae are food for oysters. Oysters are good food for drum fish. The drum is good food for you. You didn't eat the algae, yet it was an important part of your dinner!

Osprey

Plankton

Aside from providing habitats and food, oysters offer another great benefit that comes about because of the way they eat. As an oyster, you can't go to the grocery store when you're hungry because you are cemented to one spot. You wait for food particles floating in the water to flow into your shell. Instead of pizza or ice cream, you now crave **plankton** and **algae**. These animals and plants are sometimes so small that we need a microscope to see them. What else is yummy for an oyster's supper? **Detritus**. That's tiny but often nutritious bits of leaves and grass that have been washed into the water from upstream or the salt marsh. As an oyster, you'll slurp these up and then spit the water back out. If there are bits you don't want to eat like mud or sand, you'll wrap them up in a sticky goo called **mucus** and push the bundle out of your shell. Those bundled bits will now sink to the bottom of the water.

Your new way of dining may sound weird, but as an oyster you are leaving the world better than you found it.

Oysters **filter** the water as they eat, taking out particles to leave it cleaner and clearer. Once you are grown, a single oyster like you can filter as much as two and a half gallons (over 9 liters) of water per hour! This even helps with some **contaminants**, substances washed into the water that would harm the plants or animals.

The clearer water also allows more light to reach the bottom of tidal creeks and bays, helping marsh plants grow. Our salt waterways are much healthier because of oysters!

When Spartina is flooded, it serves as food for many animals and also provides shelter for them.

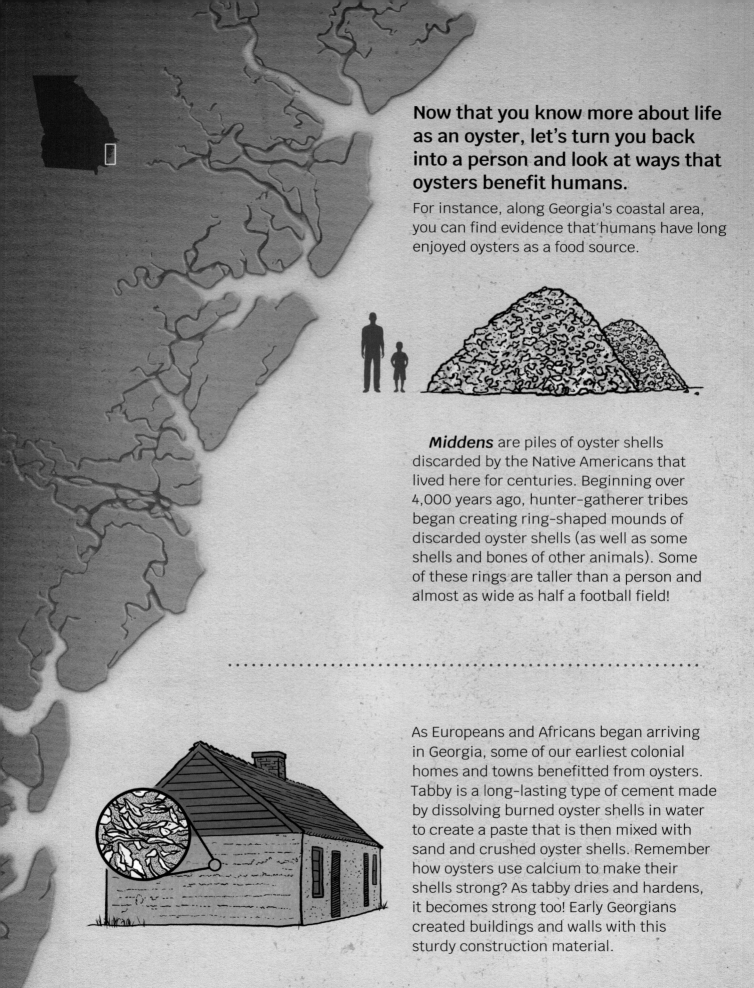

Now that you know more about life as an oyster, let's turn you back into a person and look at ways that oysters benefit humans.

For instance, along Georgia's coastal area, you can find evidence that humans have long enjoyed oysters as a food source.

Middens are piles of oyster shells discarded by the Native Americans that lived here for centuries. Beginning over 4,000 years ago, hunter-gatherer tribes began creating ring-shaped mounds of discarded oyster shells (as well as some shells and bones of other animals). Some of these rings are taller than a person and almost as wide as half a football field!

As Europeans and Africans began arriving in Georgia, some of our earliest colonial homes and towns benefitted from oysters. Tabby is a long-lasting type of cement made by dissolving burned oyster shells in water to create a paste that is then mixed with sand and crushed oyster shells. Remember how oysters use calcium to make their shells strong? As tabby dries and hardens, it becomes strong too! Early Georgians created buildings and walls with this sturdy construction material.

22

Many colonists also appreciated oysters for eating.

Georgia's oldest cookbooks have recipes for oysters roasted, baked, stewed, and even pickled!

In the early 1900s, Georgia was a leading producer of oysters and there were over a dozen canneries sealing cooked oysters in metal cans to sell far and wide.

After a while, however, there were far fewer oysters to harvest. What happened?

SHELL REMOVAL

When an oyster dies in the wild, its shells remain and spat can use them for reef building. When oysters are taken from the wild by people, most of those shells never return.

Since coastal Georgia has limited rocks and pebbles near the surface or easily accessible, people began to use crushed oyster shells for creating roads.

Ground up oyster shells are also used in chicken feed so the calcium helps create stronger eggshells.

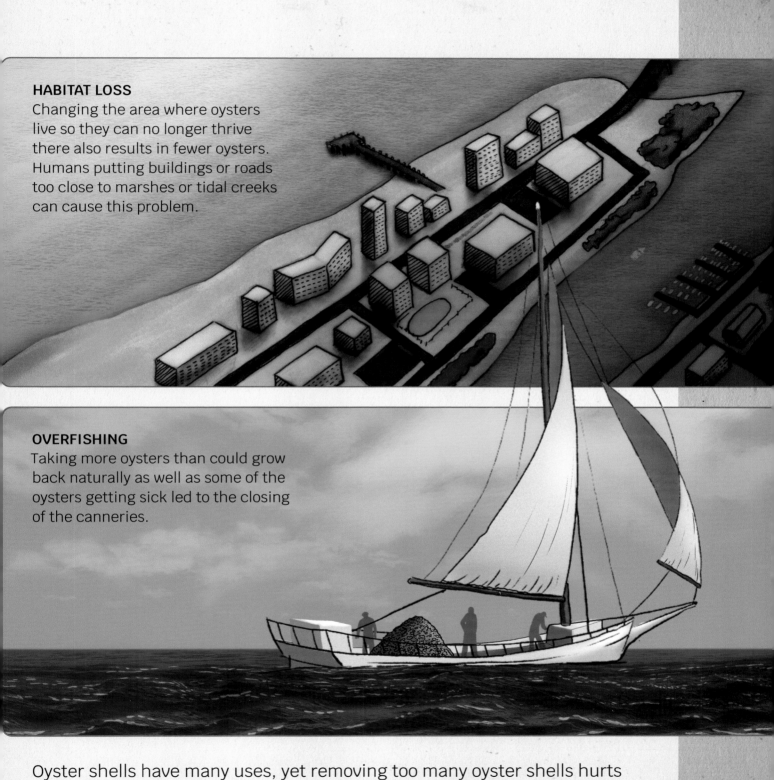

HABITAT LOSS

Changing the area where oysters live so they can no longer thrive there also results in fewer oysters. Humans putting buildings or roads too close to marshes or tidal creeks can cause this problem.

OVERFISHING

Taking more oysters than could grow back naturally as well as some of the oysters getting sick led to the closing of the canneries.

Oyster shells have many uses, yet removing too many oyster shells hurts the coastal ecosystem — the animals, the plants, and their habitats.

Like other places around the globe, Georgia now has far fewer oysters than in the past and this can lead to significant coastal changes.

One of those changes is more erosion, wind and flowing water wearing away the land. The banks of creeks and rivers sometimes change overnight if a storm batters it with rain and wind. A steep area like a creek bank may crumble away completely, killing the bushes and trees growing there. Some erosion is natural, but it can be made worse when people do not make careful choices.

Soil washes away, harming the plants that no longer have a safe place for anchoring roots or a source for the mineral nutrients they need to thrive.

What can a little wind do?

Wind blowing around **5 miles per hour** is a gentle breeze that we can feel on our faces and that ruffles the leaves on the trees. Around **15 miles per hour**, flags fly nicely on the flagpole.

25 mph Approaching 25 miles per hour, you're struggling to use an umbrella and the limbs on the trees are swaying.

35 mph At 35 miles per hour, you have trouble walking.

55 mph By 55 miles per hour, trees may be uprooted.

75 mph Hurricane-force winds are above 75 miles per hour. Hurricane Allen in 1980 had *sustained winds* (steady rather than just gusts) of over 190 miles per hour!

Strong winds push waves, making them much higher and faster. During high winds, rain, and waves, oysters help keep erosion to a healthy level on our coastline. Let's look at how they do this.

26

Remember your stroll down to the creek for fishing? Maybe you didn't know it, but you were strolling through zones or areas that are different habitats.

Oysters are often the first line of defense for all those zones. Sprawling oyster reefs help guard against too much erosion, protecting large patches of marsh and tidal creek bank.

We already know that oyster reefs are made of randomly settled oysters; this uneven surface helps break up the energy of strong waves and currents more gently than a single flat surface like a cement wall does. Even ridges of old oyster shells help protect the coastline. The animals and plants nestled around the oyster shells are sheltered.

In the *maritime climax forest zone*, you saw live oak trees and turkeys.

You placed your drink cooler in the shade of the *transitional zone* with its low bushes.

Live Oak

Red Cedar

Because the oysters help keep the creek bank safe, the low marsh won't be washed away. The roots of the plants will help hold in the soil so the high marsh above it is also safer. The clapper rail and other birds nesting in the grasses still have a home. With the lower zones now stable, the transitional zone and parts of the maritime forest are far less likely crumble into the creek or marsh.

You took the path through the *high marsh* with its sea oxeye daisies and other short plants.

Then you crossed the muddy low marsh where fiddler crabs live.

Glasswort

Smooth Cordgrass

Coastlines are places of constant change. Sands on the beach shift with each wave and tide.

Marshes grow bigger or smaller over time. One part of an island may erode away while water and wind bring sand and mud to build up another part of the same island.

Oysters help protect the coastline from too much change at once. And we can encourage oysters to grow not only in places where they once grew in large numbers but also in places where erosion endangers an important man-made building or a road.

In this book, we've explored why oysters are important. These humble (dare we even say slimy) animals are actually so significant that we call them a keystone species, and scientists are working with conservationists (people who protect habitats) to encourage more oysters to grow.

In Georgia, conservationists began teaming up with engineers in 2006 to <u>create habitats called living shorelines</u> for erosion areas.

Instead of a hardened surface — wood, rock, or cement wall to stop shoreline erosion — a slope is carefully created in the tide zone and then covered with mesh bags full of old oyster shells. In time, larval oysters settle on the shells and grow living oyster reefs.

Living shorelines do all the wonderful things natural oyster reefs do:

Slow water currents

Protect the coastline from too much erosion

Create shelter for small animals

Filter water

And the gentle slopes of living shorelines allow animals like raccoons, otters, and egrets to move freely between the land and the water. Living shorelines, in Georgia and in coastal areas around the world, support our small and squishy but necessary habitat heroes — the oysters!

Amazing Oyster Facts

- Oysters are a part of a group of animals we call *shellfish*. Bivalves like clams and mussels are shellfish, but so are *crustaceans* like shrimp, crabs, and lobsters.
- Oysters are *invertebrates*. That means they don't have a backbone. In fact, they don't have any bones!
- Oysters are *mollusks* just like snails, slugs, and octopuses.
- Most oysters begin life as males. Around their first year of life, most of them shift to being females! During warm months, males release sperm into the water while females release eggs. When the two meet up, oyster larvae begin!
- An oyster's two shells are not identical. One shell is more curved than the other. Final shell shape, however, depends on what the oyster is attached to and how many other oysters are crowded around it.
- Subtidal oysters, the ones growing completely under the water, look different than intertidal oysters even though they are the same animal. Subtidal oysters are less likely to grow in clumps, so their shells are smoother and less sharp. Restaurants prefer subtidal oysters because they can be opened more easily as well as served "on the half shell."
- Oysters have clear blood called *hemolymph*.
- Oysters in a tank can live up to 20 years. In the wild, after about three years most oysters are smothered by other oysters. If an oyster has other oysters living so close that it can no longer open its shell to filter water, it will die.

How can you help support oysters?

- If your family harvests wild oysters to eat, be careful not to take more than you are sure you are going to eat very soon. Afterwards, take the well-rinsed shells to an oyster recycling center near you. The shells will sit in a curing pile until they can be safely placed back in the water.
- Help keep our waterways clean by handling your trash responsibly. When you visit waterways, take along a bag for picking up trash and recyclables.
- Rainwater washes lawns, streets, and curbs and then flows through storm drains into wildlife areas and our waterways. Please encourage your family to be careful with oil, gasoline, soaps, *fertilizer* (plant food), *pesticides* (insect killing liquids), and *herbicides* (weed killing liquids) that could harm the environment.
- If you live in a saltwater community and you hear that a cement, metal, wood, or rock area will be put in to help save the shoreline from erosion, your family can suggest considering a living shoreline instead. Call the Georgia Department of Natural Resources for more information. If the area is outside Georgia, they can still connect you with another agency that can help.

Oyster Safety

- Oyster shells are usually sharp on the edges. Handle oyster shells carefully and always wear sturdy close-toed shoes if you are exploring areas where oysters may grow. If you get cut by an oyster, get help to carefully clean the wound.
- If your family harvests or purchases oysters for eating, check cookbooks or online guides for information about how to safely store and cook them.

Read More About Coastal Environments!

- Clayton, Tonya D. (and others). *Living with the Georgia Shore*. Durham, NC: Duke University Press, 1992.
- Lovell, Caroline Couper. *The Golden Isles of Georgia*. Atlanta: Cherokee Publishing Co., 2005.
- McKee, Gwen (editor). *A Guide to the Georgia Coast: The Georgia Conservancy*. Atlanta, Longstreet Press, 1993.
- Sherr, Evelyn B. *Marsh Mud and Mummichogs: An Intimate Natural History of Coastal Georgia*. Athens: UGA Press, 2015.
- Teal, Mildred and John. *Portrait of an Island*. Athens: UGA Press/Brown Thrasher, 1964, 1981.

Here are Information Books for Big Kids and Grownups with Lots of Pictures:

- Ballantine, Todd. *Tideland Treasure*. Columbia: USC Press, 1991.
- Bryant, David and George Davidson. *Georgia's Amazing Coast: Natural Wonders from Alligators to Zoeas*. Athens: UGA Press, 2003.
- Schoettle, Taylor. *A Guide to a Georgia Barrier Island*. St. Simons: Watermarks Publishing, 1999.
- Alber, Merryl. *And the Tide Comes In*. Taylor Trade Publishing, 2012.

Here are Some Picture Books for Younger Kids:

- Allen, Elaine Ann. *Olly the Oyster Cleans the Bay*. Centreville, MD, Tidewater Publishers, 2008.
- Dombek, Jeff. *How Oysters Saved the Bay*. Atglen, PA: Schiffer Publishing LTD, 2013.
- Downing, Johnette (illustrated by Bethanne Hill). *Why the Oyster Has the Pearl*. Gretna, LA: Pelican Publishing Company, Inc., 2011.
- Dunham, Traci (illustrated by Hannay Tuohy). *The Oyster's Secret*. Dallas: Brown Books Kids, 2017.